CROCHET
Fast & Fanciful Curling Ribbon Flowers™

General Information

Many of the products used in this pattern book may be purchased from local craft, fabric and variety stores or from the Annie's Attic Needlecraft Catalog *(see Customer Service information on page 16)*.

Contents

Primrose	2
Dogwood	3
Pansy	4
Camellia	5
Chrysanthemum	6
Rose	7
Poinsettia	8
Zinnia	9
Sunflower	10
Daffodil	11
Daisy	12
Oriental Poppy	13

Annie's Attic • Berne, IN 46711 • www.AnniesAttic.com • *Fast & Fanciful Curling Ribbon Flowers* 1

Primrose

Design by Brenda Stratton

BEGINNER

FINISHED SIZE
2⅞ inches, including Leaves

MATERIALS
- Curling ribbon (3/16 inch wide):
   10 yds blue
   3 yds green
   1 yd yellow
- Size G/6/4mm crochet hook or size needed to obtain gauge
- Tapestry needle
- Sewing needle
- Sewing thread
- Craft glue
- Pin back

GAUGE
Flower is 2¼ inches across

SPECIAL STITCH
Picot: Ch 2, sl st in 2nd ch from hook.

INSTRUCTIONS

PRIMROSE
Rnd 1: Beg at center with yellow, ch 4, 7 dc in 4th ch from hook *(first 3 chs count as first dc)*, join with sl st in 3rd ch of beg ch-4. Fasten off. *(8 dc)*

Flower Petals
Rnd 2: Join blue with sl st around post of any dc on rnd 1, [ch 2, (3 tr, hdc, 4 tr) around same post, sk next dc, sl st around post of next dc] 4 times, join with sl st in base of beg ch 2. Fasten off. *(4 petals)*

Leaves
Working behind flower petals, join green with sl st around post of any sk dc of rnd 1, (ch 3, tr, **picot** *{see Special Stitch}*, tr, ch 3, sl st) twice around post of same st, sl st around post of next sk dc of rnd 1. Fasten off. *(2 leaves)*

Arrange leaves evenly behind flower. Bring 2 opposing Flower Petals forward to overlap other 2 petals. Sew or glue pin back to back of flower. ❑❑

Dogwood

Design by Carol Alexander

EASY

FINISHED SIZE
3¼ inches, including Leaves

MATERIALS
- Curling ribbon (³⁄₁₆ inch wide):
    4 yds white
    3 yds lime green
- Size G/6/4mm crochet hook or size needed to obtain gauge
- Tapestry needle
- Sewing needle
- Sewing thread
- Opalescent lime green E beads: 10
- Craft glue
- Pin back

GAUGE
Flower is 2¼ inches across

SPECIAL STITCHES
Treble crochet cluster (tr cl): Yo twice, insert hook as indicated, yo, pull lp through, [yo, pull through 2 lps on hook] twice, yo twice, insert hook in same place, yo, pull lp through, [yo, pull through 2 lps on hook] twice, yo, pull through all lps on hook.

Double treble crochet cluster (dtr cl): Yo 3 times, insert hook as indicated, yo, pull lp through, [yo, pull through 2 lps on hook] 3 times, yo 3 times, insert hook in same place, yo, pull lp through, [yo, pull through 2 lps on hook] 3 times, yo, pull through all lps on hook.

Single crochet picot (sc picot): Ch 2, sc in top of dtr cl just made.

INSTRUCTIONS
DOGWOOD
Petals

With white, [ch 5, **tr cl** (see Special Stitches) in first ch of ch-5, ch 4, tr cl in top of last tr cl made, ch 1, sl st in same first ch *(petal made)*] 4 times. Fasten off. *(4 petals)*

Gently stretch petals slightly to smooth out, arrange evenly as shown and press with hand to help flatten.

With needle and sewing thread, sew beads in a cluster at center as shown.

LEAF
Make 2.

With lime green, ch 5, (**dtr cl**—see Special Stitches, **sc picot**—see Special Stitches, ch 4, sl st) in first ch of ch-5. Fasten off.

FINISHING
1. Sew or glue leaves to back of Dogwood as shown.
2. Sew or glue pin back to back of Dogwood.

Pansy

Design by Carol Alexander

EASY

FINISHED SIZE
3½ x 3 inches, including Leaves

MATERIALS
- Curling ribbon (3/16 inch wide):
    8 yds lavender
    5 yds green
    2 yds purple
- Size G/6/4mm crochet hook or size needed to obtain gauge
- Tapestry needle
- Sewing needle
- Sewing thread
- 6mm seed beads: 6 yellow
- Craft glue
- Pin back

GAUGE
Flower is 3 inches across

SPECIAL STITCHES
Double treble crochet cluster (dtr cl): Yo 3 times, insert hook as indicated, yo, pull lp through, [yo, pull through 2 lps on hook] 3 times, yo 3 times, insert hook in same place, yo, pull lp through, [yo, pull through 2 lps on hook] 3 times, yo, pull through all lps on hook.

Single crochet picot (sc picot): Ch 2, sc in top of dtr cl just made.

INSTRUCTIONS
PANSY
Rnd 1: With purple, ch 4, working over end of ribbon, sl st in first ch to form ring, [ch 2, 2 dc in ring, ch 2, sl st in ring] 3 times. Fasten off.
Pull end of ribbon carefully to pull center opening nearly closed, weave in end and secure on back.
Rnd 2: Join lavender with sl st in ring between any 2 petals of rnd 1, [ch 4, 3 dtr, ch 4, sl st] twice in ring *(large bottom petals)*, [ch 3, 3 dc in each of next 2 dc on next petal on rnd 1, ch 3, sl st in next sl st between petals] 3 times, working in **back lps** *(see Stitch Guide)* of large bottom petals, [ch 1, sl st in next st] across bottom petals. Fasten off.
Using photo as guide, flatten and arrange petals of rnd 2 as shown: with side petals in front of and overlapping top and bottom petals, and bottom right petal overlapping bottom left petal. Tack all overlaps securely in place to hold.
Sew or glue beads to center top petal as shown in photo.

LEAF
Make 2.
With green, ch 5, (**dtr cl**—*see Special Stitches*, **sc picot**—*see Special Stitches*, ch 4, sl st) in 5th ch from hook. Fasten off.

FINISHING
1. Sew or glue leaves to back of Pansy as shown in photo.
2. Sew or glue pin back to back of Pansy.

Camellia

Design by Carol Alexander

EASY

FINISHED SIZE
3¾ inches, including Leaves

MATERIALS
- Curling ribbon (3⁄16 inch wide):
    25 yds iridescent white
    10 yds green
- Size G/6/4mm crochet hook or size needed to obtain gauge
- Tapestry needle
- Sewing needle
- Sewing thread
- 11mm dark rose bead
- Craft glue
- Pin back

GAUGE
Flower is 3½ inches across

SPECIAL STITCHES
V-stitch (V-st): (dc, ch 2, dc) as indicated.

Single crochet picot (sc picot): Ch 2, sc around top front of **post** *(see Stitch Guide)* of last dtr made.

INSTRUCTIONS
CAMELLIA
Row 1 (RS): With iridescent white, ch 41, working in **back lps** *(see Stitch Guide)*, dc in 5th ch from hook *(first V-st)*, [ch 1, sk next 2 chs, **V-st** *(see Special Stitches)* in next ch] across, turn. *(13 V-sts)*

Row 2: Ch 3, 10 dc in ch sp of next V-st, [sl st in next ch-1 sp, 10 dc in ch sp of next V-st] across, sl st in dc of last V-st. Fasten off. *(13 petals)*

Using photo as guide, with RS facing and starting at beg of row 2 for center of flower, coil first petal into flower center, then coil rem petals fairly loosely to form 3 layers of petals as shown.

With sewing needle and thread, securely sew flower through all layers completely around and at center, weave end securely on back of flower.

Sew or glue bead to center.

LEAVES
Rnd 1: With back of flower facing, join green with sl st to center back of any outside petal, working around center area of outside flower petals, evenly space [ch 4, sl st to back of flower] 3 times to form 3½-inch wide lps, sl st in base of first ch-4, **turn.**

Rnd 2: (Sl st, ch 3, tr, 2 dtr, **sc picot**—*see Special Stitches,* dtr, tr, ch 3, sl st) in each ch sp around. Fasten off.

Sew or glue pin back to back of Camellia.

Chrysanthemum

Design by Carol Alexander

EASY

FINISHED SIZE
4½ inches, including Leaves

MATERIALS
- Curling ribbon (3/16 inch wide):
  20 yds orange
  3 yds green
  2 yds yellow
- Size G/6/4mm crochet hook or size needed to obtain gauge
- Tapestry needle
- Sewing needle
- Sewing thread
- 10mm gold bead
- Craft glue
- Pin back

GAUGE
Flower is 3¾ inches across

SPECIAL STITCHES
Treble crochet cluster (tr cl): Ch 3, yo twice, insert hook as indicated, yo, pull lp through, [yo, pull through 2 lps on hook] twice, *yo twice, insert hook in same place, yo, pull lp through, [yo, pull through 2 lps on hook] twice, rep from * once, yo, pull through all lps on hook.

Double treble crochet cluster (dtr cl): Yo 3 times, insert hook as indicated, yo, pull lp through, [yo, pull through 2 lps on hook] 3 times, yo 3 times, insert hook in same place, yo, pull lp through, [yo, pull through 2 lps on hook] 3 times, yo, pull through all lps on hook.

Single crochet picot (sc picot): Ch 2, sc in top of dtr cl just made.

INSTRUCTIONS
CHRYSANTHEMUM
Rnd 1: With yellow, ch 5, sl st in first ch to form ring, ch 1, 12 sc in ring, join with sl st in beg sc. Fasten off. *(12 sc)*

Rnd 2: Join orange with sl st in first st, ch 5 *(counts as first dc and ch 2)*, [dc in next st, ch 2] around, join with sl st in 3rd ch of ch-5. *(12 dc, 12 ch sps)*

Rnd 3: Sl st around post of first st, *ch 3, **tr cl** (see Special Stitches) in next ch sp, ch 4**, sl st around post of next st, rep from * around, ending last rep at **, join with sl st in beg sl st. Fasten off. *(12 outer petals)*

Rnd 4: Working in front of petals on last rnd, join orange with sl st around post of any dc on rnd 2, *ch 2, dc around same post, ch 2, sc around top of post of dc just made, ch 1, sl st around top of post of same dc on rnd 2**, sl st around post of next dc on rnd 2, rep from * around, ending last rep at **, join with sl st at base of beg ch-2. Fasten off. *(12 inner petals)*

Smooth inner petals and flatten against outer petals.

With sewing needle and thread, tack both rnds of petals tog invisibly along upper area of inner petals on WS as needed, leaving tips of inner petals free.

Sew or glue bead to center of flower.

LEAF
Make 2.
With green, ch 5, (**dtr cl**—see Special Stitches, **sc picot**—see Special Stitches, ch 4, sl st) in 5th ch from hook. Fasten off.

Sew or glue leaves to back of flower as shown in photo.

Sew or glue pin back to back of flower.

Rose

Design by Carol Alexander

EASY

FINISHED SIZE
3¾ inches, including Leaves

MATERIALS
- Curling ribbon (³⁄₁₆ inch wide):
   20 yds pink
   5 yds lime green
- Size G/6/4mm crochet hook or size needed to obtain gauge
- Tapestry needle
- Sewing needle
- Sewing thread
- ¾-inch decorative shank button
- Craft glue
- Pin back

GAUGE
Flower is 3 inches across

SPECIAL STITCHES
Extended double crochet (edc): Yo, insert hook in st indicated, yo, pull lp through, yo, pull through 1 lp on hook, [yo, pull through 2 lps on hook] twice.

Double treble crochet cluster (dtr cl): Yo 3 times, insert hook as indicated, yo, pull lp through, [yo, pull through 2 lps on hook] 3 times, yo 3 times, insert hook in same place, yo, pull lp through, [yo, pull through 2 lps on hook] 3 times, yo, pull through all lps on hook.

Single crochet picot (sc picot): Ch 2, sc in top of dtr cl just made.

INSTRUCTIONS
ROSE
Rnd 1: With pink, ch 4, sl st in first ch to form ring, working over end, ch 6 (counts as first edc and ch 2), [edc (see Special Stitches) in ring, ch 2] 7 times, join with sl st in 4th ch of beg ch-6. (8 edc, 8 ch sps)

Rnd 2: Working around top half of post of each edc on rnd 1, ch 1, (sc, ch 1, 5 tr, ch 1, sc) around post of each edc around, join with sl st in beg sc. (8 outer petals)

Rnd 3: Working around bottom half of post of each edc on rnd 1, (sc, 3 dc, sc) around post of each edc around, join with sl st in beg sc. Fasten off. (8 inner petals)

Flatten and smooth all petals, arranging evenly with petals slightly overlapping in pinwheel fashion as shown.

Pull beg ribbon end gently to slightly close center opening, weave in end and secure to back.

Sew or glue button to center of rose.

LEAVES
Working behind outer petals, join lime green with sl st in any ch-2 sp of rnd 1, ch 4, (**dtr cl**—see Special Stitches, **sc picot**—see Special Stitches, ch 4, sl st) in same ch sp, (sl st, ch 4, dtr cl, sc picot, ch 4, sl st) in each of next 2 ch sps. Fasten off.

Sew or glue pin back to back of Rose.

Poinsettia

Design adapted by Brenda Stratton from an Annie Potter Original

EASY

FINISHED SIZE
6¼ inches, including Leaves

MATERIALS
- Curling ribbon (3⁄16 inch wide):
   30 yds red
   10 yds green
- Size G/6/4mm crochet hook or size needed to obtain gauge
- Tapestry needle
- Sewing needle
- Sewing thread
- 7⁄8-inch gold shank nugget button
- Craft glue
- Pin back

GAUGE
Flower is 6 inches across

INSTRUCTIONS
POINSETTIA
Make 2.
Rnd 1: With red, ch 2, 5 sc in 2nd ch from hook, join with sl st in beg sc. *(5 sc)*
Rnd 2: Ch 1, sc in first st, ch 3, [sc in next st, ch 3] around, join.

First Petal
Row 3: Now working in rows, (sl st, ch 3—*counts as first dc*, 4 dc) in first ch sp, leaving rem ch sps unworked, turn. *(5 dc)*
Row 4: Ch 3, dc in each st across, turn.
Row 5: Ch 2 *(does not count as first dc)*, dc in each of next 2 sts, **dc dec** *(see Stitch Guide)* in last 2 sts, turn. *(3 dc)*
Row 6: Ch 2, dc dec in last 2 sts, ch 1, sl st in top of dc dec just made. Fasten off.

Second Petal
Row 3: Join red with sl st in next unworked ch sp on rnd 2, ch 3, 4 dc in same ch sp, turn. *(5 dc)*
Row 4: Ch 3, dc in each st across, turn.
Row 5: Ch 2 *(does not count as first dc)*, dc in each of next 2 sts, dc dec in last 2 sts, turn. *(3 dc)*
Row 6: Ch 2, dc dec in last 2 sts, ch 1, sl st in top of dc dec just made. Fasten off.

Remaining Petals
Rep rows 3–6 of Second Petal.

LEAF
Make 3.
Beg at base of leaf with green, ch 9, 2 sc in 2nd ch from hook, hdc in next ch, dc in each of next 4 chs, hdc in next ch, (sc, ch 1, sc) in last ch, working on opposite side of ch, hdc in next ch, dc in each of next 4 chs, hdc in next ch, sc in same ch as beg 2 sc, join with sl st in beg sc. Fasten off.

ASSEMBLY
1. Position 1 Poinsettia on top of the other, rotating the top Poinsettia slightly so Petals are offset. Sew or glue in place at center
2. Glue button to center of flower.
3. Sew or glue Leaves to back of flower as shown in photo.
4. Sew or glue pin back to back of flower.

Zinnia

Design by Patricia Hall

EASY

FINISHED SIZE
5¾ inches, including Leaves

MATERIALS
- Curling ribbon (³⁄₁₆ inch wide):
  30 yds fuchsia
  10 yds yellow
  10 yds green
- Size G/6/4mm crochet hook or size needed to obtain gauge
- Tapestry needle
- Sewing needle
- Sewing thread
- Craft glue
- Pin back

GAUGE
Flower is 4 inches across

PATTERN NOTE
Do not join rounds unless otherwise stated. Mark first stitch of each round.

INSTRUCTIONS
ZINNIA
Rnd 1: With yellow, ch 2, 5 sc in 2nd ch from hook, **do not join** (see Pattern Note). (5 sc)
Rnd 2: 2 sc in each st around. (10 sc)
Rnd 3: Working in **back lps** (see Stitch Guide), 2 sc in each st around. (20 sc)
Rnd 4: Working in back lps, sc in each st around.
Rnd 5: Working in back lps, [sc in next st, 2 sc in next st] around. (30 sc)
Rnd 6: Working in back lps, sc in each st around, join with sl st in beg sc. Fasten off.

Petals
Working in front lps, join fuchsia with sc in any st of rnd 2, (ch 2, dc, ch 2, sc) in same st, (sc, ch 2, dc, ch 2, sc) in each st around, continue to work in each st around rnds 3–5. At end of last rnd, join with sl st in beg sc of first petal on rnd 5. Fasten off.

LEAF
Make 3.
With green, ch 10, sl st in 2nd ch from hook, sc in next ch, hdc in next ch, dc in next ch, 2 dc in next ch, dc in each of next 2 chs, hdc in next ch, (sc, ch 2, sc) in end ch, working on opposite side of ch, hdc in next ch, dc in each of next 2 chs, 2 dc in next ch, dc in next ch, hdc in next ch, sc in next ch, sl st in last ch. Fasten off.

FINISHING
1. Sew or glue leaves to back of flower according to photo.
2. Sew or glue pin back to back of flower.

Sunflower

Design by Patricia Hall

EASY

FINISHED SIZE
5½ inches, including Leaves

MATERIALS
- Curling ribbon (3/16 inch wide):
  20 yds golden yellow
  10 yds green
- Size G/6/4mm crochet hook or size needed to obtain gauge
- Tapestry needle
- Sewing needle
- Sewing thread
- 1-inch brown shank button
- Craft glue
- Pin back

GAUGE
Flower is 4½ inches across

SPECIAL STITCH
Picot: Ch 2, sl st in top of last st made.

INSTRUCTIONS

SUNFLOWER
Rnd 1: With golden yellow, ch 4, sl st in first ch to form ring, ch 2 *(counts as first hdc)*, 13 hdc in ring, join with sl st in top of beg ch-2. *(14 hdc)*

Rnd 2: Ch 3, sk next st, [sc in next st, ch 3, sk next st] around, join with sl st in beg sc. *(7 ch sps)*

Rnd 3: Sl st in first ch sp, ch 1, (sc, ch 2, dc, tr, **picot**—*see Special Stitch*, dc, ch 2, sc) in same ch sp and in each ch sp around, join. *(7 petals)*

Rnd 4: Working behind rnd 3 in sk sts of rnd 1, ch 4, [sc in next st, ch 4] around, join.

Rnd 5: Sl st in first ch sp, ch 1, (sc, ch 3, tr, dtr, picot, tr, ch 3, sc) in same ch sp and in each ch sp around, join. Fasten off.

Sew or glue button to center of flower.

LEAF
Make 3.
With green, ch 8, sc in 2nd ch from hook, hdc in next ch, dc in each of next 3 chs, hdc in next ch, sc in end ch, **for tip**, ch 3, sc in 2nd ch from hook, sc in next ch, working on opposite side of starting ch, sc in next ch, hdc in next ch, dc in each of next 3 chs, hdc in next ch, sc in last ch, join with sl st in beg sc. Fasten off.

FINISHING
1. Sew or glue Leaves to back of flower as shown in photo.
2. Sew or glue pin back to back of flower.

Daffodil

Design by Patricia Hall

EASY

FINISHED SIZE
4½ inches, including Leaves

MATERIALS
- Curling ribbon (3/16 inch wide):
  25 yds yellow
  5 yds green
- Size F/5/3.75mm crochet hook or size needed to obtain gauge
- Tapestry needle
- Sewing needle
- Sewing thread
- 6mm multifaceted beads: 3 orange
- Craft glue
- Pin back

GAUGE
Flower is 4 inches across

SPECIAL STITCHES
Treble crochet cluster (tr cl): Yo twice, insert hook as indicated, yo, pull lp through, [yo, pull through 2 lps on hook] twice, *yo twice, insert hook in same place, yo, pull lp through, [yo, pull through 2 lps on hook] twice, rep from * once, yo, pull through all lps on hook.

Double treble crochet cluster (dtr cl): Yo 3 times, insert hook as indicated, yo, pull lp through, [yo, pull through 2 lps on hook] 3 times, yo 3 times, insert hook in same place, yo, pull lp through, [yo, pull through 2 lps on hook] 3 times, yo, pull through all lps on hook.

Single crochet picot (sc picot): Ch 2, sc in top of dtr cl just made.

INSTRUCTIONS
DAFFODIL
Front
Rnd 1: With yellow, ch 4, sl st in first ch to form ring, ch 3 (*counts as first dc*), 15 dc in ring, join with sl st in 3rd ch of beg ch-3. (*16 dc*)

Rnd 2: Working in **back lps** (*see Stitch Guide*) this rnd, ch 1, 2 sc in first st, sc in next st, [2 sc in next st, sc in next st] around, join with sl st in beg sc. (*24 sc*)

Rnd 3: *Ch 3, **tr cl** (*see Special Stitches*), ch 3**, sl st in each of next 2 sts, rep from * around, ending last rep at **, sl st in last st, join with sl st in base of beg ch-3. (*6 tr cls*)

Rnd 4: Ch 1, sk all sl sts, *(sl st, 3 sc) in next ch sp, (sc, ch 2, sc) in next cl, (3 sc, sl st) in next ch sp, rep from * around, join with sl st in beg sl st. Fasten off.

Rnd 5: Working this rnd in front lps of rnd 1, with petals facing, join yellow with sl st in any st of rnd 1, ch 3 (*counts as first dc*), dc in each st around, join with sl st in 3rd ch of beg ch-3. (*16 dc*)

Rnd 6: [Ch 3, sl st in next st] around, ch 3, join with sl st in base of beg ch-3. Fasten off.

LEAF
Make 3.
With green, ch 5, (**dtr cl**—*see Special Stitches*, **sc picot**—*see Special Stitches,* ch 4, sl st) in 5th ch from hook. Fasten off.

FINISHING
1. Sew or glue Leaves to back of flower as shown in photo.
2. Sew or glue beads to center of flower.
3. Sew or glue pin back to back of flower.

Daisy

Design by Brenda Stratton

EASY

FINISHED SIZE
4 inches, including Leaves

MATERIALS
- Curling ribbon (3/16 inch wide):
    25 yds white
    10 yds green
- Size G/6/4mm crochet hook or size needed to obtain gauge
- Tapestry needle
- Sewing needle
- Sewing thread
- 7/8-inch yellow shank button
- Craft glue
- Pin back

GAUGE
Flower is 3½ inches across

INSTRUCTIONS

DAISY
Center
Rnd 1: With white, ch 4, sl st in first ch to form ring, ch 1, 12 sc in ring, join with a sl st in first sc. *(12 sc)*

Petals
Rnd 2: Ch 6, sl st in 2nd ch from hook and in each of next 2 chs, hdc in next ch, sc in next ch, [sl st in next sc of rnd 1, ch 6, sl st in 2nd ch from hook and in each of next 2 chs, hdc in next ch, sc in next ch] 11 times, join with a sl st in beg sl st. *(12 petals)*

Rnd 3: Working around outer edges of all petals, [sl st in each of next 5 sts on petal, (sl st, ch 1, sl st) in tip of Petal, sl st in each of next 5 sts on opposite side of petal, sl st in next sc in rnd 1] around. Fasten off.

LEAF
Make 2.
Row 1: Beg at base of leaf with green, ch 9, sl st in 2nd ch from hook, sc in each of next 6 chs, sl st in last ch. Do not turn. *(8 sts)*

Rnd 2: Now working in rnds around outer edge of leaf, ch 1, sl st in same st as last sl st in row 1, sl st in base of each of next 6 sc, (sl st, ch 1, sl st) in next sc at tip; now working down opposite side of leaf, sl st in each of next 6 sc, sl st in beg sl st. Fasten off. *(16 sl sts)*

FINISHING
1. Overlap base ends of Leaves; sew or glue ends of Leaves to back of Daisy at base of Petals as shown in photo.
2. Sew or glue yellow button to center front of Daisy.
3. Sew or glue pin back to center back of Daisy.

Oriental Poppy

Design by Brenda Stratton

EASY

FINISHED SIZE
6 inches, including Leaves

MATERIALS
- Curling ribbon (³⁄₁₆ inch wide):
    25 yds red
    10 yds green
- Lion Brand Fun Fur bulky (chunky) weight eyelash yarn (1½ oz/60 yds/40g per skein):
    2 yds #153 black
- Size G/6/4mm crochet hook or size needed to obtain gauge
- Tapestry needle
- Sewing needle
- Sewing thread
- Craft glue
- Pin back

GAUGE
Flower is 4¼ inches across

INSTRUCTIONS

POPPY
Center
Rnd 1: With red, ch 4, sl st in first ch to form ring, ch 1, 6 sc in ring, **do not join**. *(6 sc)*
Rnd 2: 2 sc in each st around, join with sl st in beg sc. *(12 sc)*
Rnd 3: Ch 1, sc in first st, ch 3, sk next st, [sc in next st, ch 3, sk next st] around, join. *(6 ch sps)*

Top Layer of Petals
First Petal
Row 1: Now working in rows, sl st to ch-3 sp, ch 1, (sc, 6 hdc, sc) in same ch sp, leaving rem ch sps unworked, turn.
Row 2: Ch 1, sc in first sc, 2 hdc in each of next 6 hdc, sc in next sc, turn.
Row 3: Ch 1, sc in first st, ch 2, [sc in next st, ch 2] across with sc in last st, sk next ch-3 sp of rnd 3 of Center, with sk ch-3 sp at back, sl st in next ch-3 sp, **do not turn**.

Second Petal
Work same as First Petal.

Third Petal
Row 1: Now working in rows, sl st to ch-3 sp, ch 1, (sc, 6 hdc, sc) in same ch sp, leaving rem ch sps unworked, turn.
Row 2: Ch 1, sc in first sc, 2 hdc in each of next 6 hdc, sc in next sc, turn.
Row 3: Ch 1, sc in first st, ch 3, [sc in next st, ch 3] across with sc in last st, join with sl st in beg sc of First Petal. Fasten off.

Bottom Layer of Petals
Fourth–Sixth Petals
Working in sk ch-3 sps on rnd 3 of Center behind Petals, join with sc in first ch sp and work same as First–Third Petals.

Leaf
Make 3.
Beg at base, with green, ch 9, 2 sc in 2nd ch from hook, hdc in next ch, dc in each of next 4 chs, hdc in next ch, (sc, ch 1, sc) in last ch, working on opposite side of ch, hdc in next ch, dc in each of next 4 chs, hdc in next ch, sc in same ch as beg 2 sc, join with sl st in beg sc. Fasten off.

Stamens
Rnd 1: With black eyelash yarn, ch 4, join to form ring; ch 3, 15 dc in ring, join. Fasten off. *(16 dc)*

FINISHING
1. Arrange Petals as desired.
2. Glue base of Leaves to back of Petals as shown in photo.
3. Sew or glue Stamens to center front of Poppy as shown.
4. Sew or glue pin back to back of Poppy.

Stitch Guide

ABBREVIATIONS

beg	begin/beginning
bpdc	back post double crochet
bpsc	back post single crochet
bptr	back post treble crochet
CC	contrasting color
ch	chain stitch
ch-	refers to chain or space previously made (i.e. ch-1 space)
ch sp	chain space
cl	cluster
cm	centimeter(s)
dc	double crochet
dec	decrease/decreases/decreasing
dtr	double treble crochet
fpdc	front post double crochet
fpsc	front post single crochet
fptr	front post treble crochet
g	gram(s)
hdc	half double crochet
inc	increase/increases/increasing
lp(s)	loop(s)
MC	main color
mm	millimeter(s)
oz	ounce(s)
pc	popcorn
rem	remain/remaining
rep	repeat(s)
rnd(s)	round(s)
RS	right side
sc	single crochet
sk	skip(ped)
sl st	slip stitch
sp(s)	space(s)
st(s)	stitch(es)
tog	together
tr	treble crochet
trtr	triple treble
WS	wrong side
yd(s)	yard(s)
yo	yarn over

Chain—ch: Yo, pull through lp on hook.

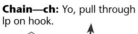

Slip stitch—sl st: Insert hook in st, yo, pull through both lps on hook.

Single crochet—sc: Insert hook in st, yo, pull through st, yo, pull through both lps on hook.

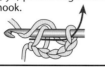

Front loop—front lp
Back loop—back lp

Front post stitch—fp: Back post stitch—bp: When working post st, insert hook from right to left around post st on previous row.

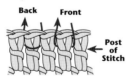

Half double crochet—hdc: Yo, insert hook in st, yo, pull through st, yo, pull through all 3 lps on hook.

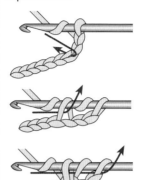

Double crochet—dc: Yo, insert hook in st, yo, pull through st, [yo, pull through 2 lps] twice.

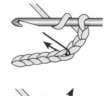

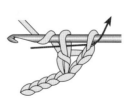

Change colors: Drop first color; with second color, pull through last 2 lps of st.

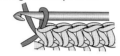

Treble crochet—tr: Yo twice, insert hook in st, yo, pull through st, [yo, pull through 2 lps] 3 times.

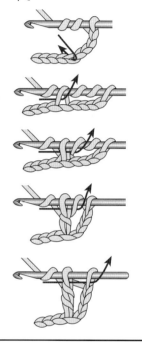

Double treble crochet—dtr: Yo 3 times, insert hook in st, yo, pull through st, [yo, pull through 2 lps] 4 times.

Single crochet decrease (sc dec): (Insert hook, yo, draw up a lp) in each of the sts indicated, yo, draw through all lps on hook.

Example of 2-sc dec

Half double crochet decrease (hdc dec): (Yo, insert hook, yo, draw lp through) in each of the sts indicated, yo, draw through all lps on hook.

Example of 2-hdc dec

Double crochet decrease (dc dec): (Yo, insert hook, yo, draw lp through, yo, draw through 2 lps on hook) in each of the sts indicated, yo, draw through all lps on hook.

Example of 2-dc dec

US		UK
sl st (slip stitch)	=	sc (single crochet)
sc (single crochet)	=	dc (double crochet)
hdc (half double crochet)	=	htr (half treble crochet)
dc (double crochet)	=	tr (treble crochet)
tr (treble crochet)	=	dtr (double treble crochet)
dtr (double treble crochet)	=	ttr (triple treble crochet)
skip	=	miss

For more complete information, visit

StitchGuide.com

306 East Parr Road
Berne, IN 46711
© 2005 Annie's Attic

TOLL-FREE ORDER LINE or to request a free catalog (800) LV-ANNIE (800) 582-6643
Customer Service (800) AT-ANNIE (800) 282-6643, **Fax** (800) 882-6643
Visit www.AnniesAttic.com

We have made every effort to ensure the accuracy and completeness of these instructions.
We cannot, however, be responsible for human error, typographical mistakes or variations in individual work.
Reprinting or duplicating the information, photographs or graphics in this publication by any means,
including copy machine, computer scanning, digital photography, e-mail, personal Web site and fax,
is illegal. Failure to abide by federal copyright laws may result in litigation and fines.

ISBN: 1-59635-032-6   All rights reserved   Printed in USA   2 3 4 5 6 7 8 9